MW00655420

Reach For Prosperity

- ❑ *You Will Never Possess Anything You Are Unwilling To Pursue.*

- ❑ It is good to pursue good health, happiness and financial blessings. Your Heavenly Father wants you to experience all these blessings.

- ❑ Get ready today to launch the greatest chapter you have ever known: PROSPERITY.

The Word

"Beloved, I wish above all things that thou mayest prosper and be in health, even as thy soul prospereth."

(3 John 1:2)

2

Stay In The Center of Your Expertise

- ❑ *Even In Your Mother's Womb You Were Given By God Special Gifts, Talents And Skills.*

- ❑ *What you enjoy doing the most is a clue to what God wants you to do with your life.*

- ❑ Start today to build your *daily agenda* around this Assignment.

The Word

"Let every man abide in the same calling wherein he was called."

(1 Corinthians 7:20)

3

DO WHAT YOU LOVE

- ❑ *Whatever Brings You The Most Fulfillment Is An Important Key To Your Life.*

- ❑ God wants you happy. That is a settled issue. Now find what makes you happy.

- ❑ *You will have extraordinary success with something that becomes your obsession.*

The Word

"Wherefore I perceive that there is nothing better, than that a man should rejoice in his own works; for that is his portion: for who shall bring him to see what shall be after him?"

(Ecclesiastes 3:22)

4

Pinpoint Your Needs

- ❑ *List Your Personal Financial Needs.* These may include money for your home, your children's education or whatever.

- ❑ *Your faith will begin to respond to this specific target.*

- ❑ Now, hold this list before the Lord. *Wrap your faith around it* and watch Jehovah-Jireh, your Provider, begin to move in your life.

The Word

"But my God shall supply all your need according to His riches in glory by Christ Jesus." (Philippians 4:19)

5

BECOME DEBT-FREE

- ❑ *Financial Pressure Is Devastating To A Marriage And Family.* It is considered the major cause of divorce.

- ❑ *Make a list* of all your debts today.

- ❑ Now, focus your faith and efforts toward moving this mountain. Your life is worth it.

The Word

"The rich ruleth over the poor, and the borrower is servant to the lender."

(Proverbs 22:7)

6

ASK THE GIVER

- *Everything Comes From Somebody.*
- Whatever you need...*already exists.*
- *Ask.* Ask with *joy.* Somebody wants to reveal His Power to you.

The Word

"Or what man is there of you, whom if his son ask bread, will he give him a stone? Or if he ask a fish, will he give him a serpent? If ye then, being evil, know how to give good gifts unto your children, how much more shall your Father which is in Heaven give good things to them that ask Him?"

(Matthew 7:9-11)

7

CONSULT THE LEARNED

- *The Difference Between Today And Your Future Is Information.*
- If you do not learn anything new today, tomorrow will be just like today. This means you do not have a future...just a *longer* today.
- So, read...listen...observe. *Your future is in your discoveries.*

The Word

"Where no counsel is, the people fall: but in the multitude of counsellors there is safety." (Proverbs 11:14)

8

THINK AHEAD

- ❑ *I Call It "The Law of Inevitable Eventuality."*

- ❑ If you eat two slices of pecan pie every night, what is the inevitable eventually? If you smoke two packs of cigarettes a day, what is the inevitable eventuality?

- ❑ Whatever you are doing right now...is producing an inevitable future. Think, think, think...ahead.

The Word

"Go to the ant, thou sluggard; consider her ways, and be wise Which having no guide, overseer, or ruler, Provideth her meat in the summer, and gathereth her food in the harvest." (Proverbs 6:6-8)

9

DISCOVER YOUR REAL SOURCE

- ❑ *You Do Not Have A Thing God Did Not Give You.*

- ❑ Never forget it. Do not get cocky and arrogant about the little 10 percent tithe you give to God. He is the one that gave the 100 percent you have.

- ❑ *He is your Total Source.* He knows it. Champions know it, too.

The Word

"And when thy herds and thy flocks multiply, and thy silver and thy gold is multiplied, and all that thou hast is multiplied; But thou shalt remember the Lord thy God: for it is He that giveth thee power to get wealth, that He may establish His covenant which He sware unto thy fathers, as it is this day."

(Deuteronomy 8:13, 18)

10

DO NOT RUSH IT

- ❑ *Great Things Take Time.*
- ❑ Human pregnancy takes 9 months. Jesus' preparation for ministry took 30 years.
- ❑ Willingly pace yourself on the Journey to Prosperity. Your present joy depends on it.

11

KEEP GOOD RECORDS

- ❑ *Accountability Is Vital In Today's World.*
- ❑ Balance your checkbook *regularly.* Keep necessary *receipts* of your purchases.
- ❑ *Information that is not retrievable is not usable.* Keep clean records.

The Word

"He that hasteth to be rich hath an evil eye, and considereth not that poverty shall come upon him." (Proverbs 28:22)

12

TITHE WITH EXPECTATION

- ❑ *Tithe Means "Tenth."* Abraham brought 10 percent of his income back to God in thanksgiving for the blessing of God.
- ❑ This tithe is "Holy Seed."
- ❑ As you bring your tithes to God this week, wrap your faith and *expectation* around it and *look for the promised Harvest.*

The Word

"Bring ye all the tithes into the storehouse, that there may be meat in Mine house, and prove Me now herewith, saith the Lord of hosts, if I will not open you the windows of Heaven, and pour you out a blessing, that there shall not be room enough to receive it. And I will rebuke the devourer for your sakes, and he shall not destroy the fruits of your ground." (Malachi 3:10-11)

13

CELEBRATE YOUR SEED

- ❑ *It Is Thrilling That Offering Time Is Becoming A Happy And Joyous Occasion In Many Churches Today.*

- ❑ Many knowledgeable pastors are even "Celebrating The Seed"...by having their entire congregation bring their tithes and offerings forward to the altar each Sunday morning.

- ❑ Celebrate your Seed. Your Father does.

The Word

"For the seed shall be prosperous; the vine shall give her fruit, and the ground shall give her increase, and the Heavens shall give their dew; and I will cause the remnant of this people to possess all these things." (Zechariah 8:12)

14

STOP SPENDING MORE THAN YOU EARN

- ❑ *It Is Possible To Live On Less And Still Be Happy.*

- ❑ The missing ingredient in much "prosperity teaching" is...*temperance* in all things.

- ❑ *Buying on credit is merely stripping your future to enhance your present.* Slow down and start living within your means.

The Word

"And every man that striveth for the mastery is temperate in all things. Now they do it to obtain a corruptible crown; but we an incorruptible."

(1 Corinthians 9:25)

15

Do Not Waste Time

- ❑ *Time Is Precious.* It is life itself. When you waste your time, you are wasting your life.

- ❑ *Managing your time wisely* is one of the most important keys to financial prosperity.

- ❑ Keep a *written list* of your daily tasks. Link each task to a *specific time.* This creates order—the accurate arrangement of things. *It is the Power Key to Productivity.*

The Word

"Redeeming the time, because the days are evil." (Ephesians 5:16)

16

DO NOT MAKE QUICK DECISIONS

- ❑ *Your Entire Life Hinges On The Decisions You Make.*
- ❑ Your decisions will create tragedies or joy. Laughter or tears. Pain or pleasure.
- ❑ Do not let anyone rush you into any decision before you are prepared. Be patient. *Remember, patience is the weapon that forces deception to reveal itself.*

The Word

"Wherefore, my beloved brethren, let every man be swift to hear, slow to speak, slow to wrath." (James 1:19)

17

Honor Your Word

- ❑ *Truth Is The Most Powerful Force On Earth. It cannot be changed.*
- ❑ Be honest. Cherish your integrity. Keep your word.
- ❑ *Never make a promise impossible to keep.*

The Word

"A good name is rather to be chosen than great riches, and loving favour rather than silver and gold." (Proverbs 22:1)

18

BRAINSTORM FOR CREATIVE IDEAS

- ❑ *God Has Countless And Varied Ways To Get Finances Into Your Hands.*

- ❑ Sit down today with two creative friends. Together, pray for God to give you the greatest financial ideas you have ever birthed.

- ❑ Write them down. *God will teach you to profit.*

The Word

"Thus saith the Lord, thy Redeemer, the Holy One of Israel; I am the Lord thy God which teacheth thee to profit, which leadeth thee by the way that thou shouldest go." (Isaiah 48:17)

19

Be Faithful In The Little Things

- ❑ *Little Hinges Swing Big Doors.* Acorns produce oak trees.

- ❑ *Little things really do matter.* Develop a passion for *details.*

- ❑ Just do the basics: keep a budget, balance your checkbook, pay your bills on time, plant your Seeds in the work of God, *expect to see miracles every day of your life.*

The Word

"His lord said unto him, Well done, good and faithful servant; thou hast been faithful over a few things, I will make thee ruler over many things: enter thou into the joy of thy lord."

(Matthew 25:23)

20

STAY HEALTHY

- *Energy Is A Major Ingredient For Success.*

- Respect your body. Listen to it. *When Fatigue Walks In, Faith Walks Out.*

- A well-known doctor, famous for treating depression patients, said he had never had a depressed patient who was really physically fit. *What you spend your time on is what you truly respect.*

The Word

"And ye shall serve the Lord your God, and he shall bless thy bread, and thy water; and I will take sickness away from the midst of thee." (Exodus 23:25)

21

Network With Others

- ❑ *Remember, One Cannot Multiply.*
- ❑ Develop people-skills. Listen. Absorb from others. Ask questions. Document answers.
- ❑ *Success is a collection of relationships.* Whatever you are willing to settle for, determines the *quality of your future.*

The Word

"Two are better than one; because they have a good reward for their labour. For if they fall, the one will lift up his fellow: but woe to him that is alone when he falleth; for he hath not another to help him up." (Ecclesiastes 4:9-10)

22

DRAW UP A DETAILED PLAN

- ❑ *Your Vision Is Your Future.*

- ❑ The Bible is God's written List of Goals. He wrote down what He wanted to happen.

- ❑ It may be difficult for you to transfer your thoughts on paper, but do it. *Something wonderful starts happening when you actually see a blueprint of your future.*

The Word

"And the Lord answered me, and said, Write the vision, and make it plain upon tables, that he may run that readeth it."
(Habakkuk 2:2)

"Where there is no vision, the people perish: but he that keepeth the law, happy is he." (Proverbs 29:18)

23

DETERMINE TO BE DILIGENT

- ❑ *Diligence Is Speedy Attention To An Assigned Task.*

- ❑ Respond *immediately* to your supervisor's instructions. Do not wait. *Act.*

- ❑ According to the Bible, this is a key element to every promotion. So, move... move...move quickly to your assigned tasks.

The Word

"He becometh poor that dealeth with a slack hand: but the hand of the diligent maketh rich." (Proverbs 10:4)

24

DO NOT WASTE MONEY

- ❑ You Often Hear That Billionaires Are Stingy. Some are even known to bring their own lunch to work. They learned early to make every dollar count.

- ❑ What you do with $10 is what you will eventually do with $100.

- ❑ Respect what God has given you. What you do not respect, you will eventually lose.

The Word

"Not slothful in business; fervent in spirit; serving the Lord." (Romans 12:11)

25

Go The Extra Mile

- ❑ *Jesus Taught "The Law of The Second Mile."*
- ❑ It simply means to do *more* than what is really expected of you. It means to *think* and *look* for *extra* ways to *benefit* others.
- ❑ Always remember—*Your rewards are determined by the kinds of problems you are willing to solve.*

The Word

"And whosoever shall compel thee to go a mile, go with him twain."

(Matthew 5:41)

26

PURSUE WISDOM

- ❑ *Wisdom Is Simply Doing What God Would Do In A Given Situation.*

- ❑ Wisdom is the Master Key to financial prosperity.

- ❑ Jesus is made unto us the Wisdom of God. Whatever you face today, *just do what you know Jesus would do.*

The Word

"Get Wisdom, get understanding: forget it not; neither decline from the words of my mouth." (Proverbs 4:5)

"Length of days is in her right hand; and in her left hand riches and honour." (Proverbs 3:16)

27

FEAR GOD

- ❑ *To Fear God Does Not Mean To Be Afraid of God.* It means to *respect, honor and complete any instruction He gives you.*

- ❑ Your obedience *triggers events* that bring financial blessings. Disobedience triggers events that bring financial ruin.

- ❑ *The fear of the Lord is the beginning of Wisdom.*

The Word

"By humility and the fear of the Lord are riches, and honour, and life."

(Proverbs 22:4)

28

DO NOT ATTEMPT TOO MANY THINGS

- *A Famous Billionaire Once Said, "I've Seen As Many People Fail From Attempting Too Many Things As I Have From Attempting Too Few."*

- Do not overload yourself. It will *break your focus.*

- *The Real Reason Men Fail Is Broken Focus.* Find something *worthy* of consuming you, and *pour your life into it.*

The Word

"A double minded man is unstable in all his ways." (James 1:8)

29

Look For A Problem To Solve

- ❑ *Everything God Has Made Is A Solution To A Problem.*

- ❑ *Your worth and significance are determined by the kinds of problems you are solving for someone.* If you want to earn $100 an hour, you must find a $100 an hour problem to solve.

- ❑ Your significance is not your similarity to others. It is your *difference.* Find your *point of difference...*and *solve a problem with it.* Prosperity is inevitable.

The Word

"Withhold not good from them to whom it is due, when it is in the power of thine hand to do it." (Proverbs 3:27)

30

REMEMBER THE POOR

- ❑ *Thousands Are Homeless, Destitute And Impoverished.*
- ❑ *Your reaction to them determines God's reaction to you.*
- ❑ Get involved. Plant your best Seed in a church or worthy organization committed to the poor. Your own prosperity will be affected by it.

The Word

"Blessed is he that considereth the poor: the Lord will deliver him in time of trouble. The Lord will preserve him, and keep him alive; and he shall be blessed upon the earth: and thou wilt not deliver him unto the will of his enemies."

(Psalm 41:1-2)

31

ENLARGE YOUR CORNER

- *God Instructed The Wealthy To Leave Barley And Wheat In The Corners of Their Fields For The Poor And Needy.*
- Your *field* is anything God has given to you. Your *corner* is anything you are giving back to God.
- Your field is your *income.* Your corner is your *outgo. The larger you make your corner, the larger God will make your field.* It is just a matter of *time.*

The Word

"And when ye reap the harvest of your land, thou shalt not wholly reap the corners of thy field, neither shalt thou gather the gleanings of thy harvest. And thou shalt not glean thy vineyard, neither shalt thou gather every grape of thy vineyard; thou shalt leave them for the poor and stranger: I am the Lord your God." (Leviticus 19:9-10)

Clip & Mail

DECISION

Will You Accept Jesus As Your Personal Savior Today?

The Bible says, "That if thou shalt confess with thy mouth the Lord Jesus, and shalt believe in thine heart that God hath raised Him from the dead, thou shalt be saved," (Romans 10:9).

Pray this prayer from your heart today! *"Dear Jesus, I believe that You died for me and rose again on the third day. I confess I am a sinner...I need Your love and forgiveness...Come into my heart. Forgive my sins. I receive Your eternal life. Confirm Your love by giving me peace, joy and supernatural love for others. Amen."*

☐ Yes, Mike! I made a decision to accept Christ as my personal Savior today. Please send me my free gift of your book *31 Keys to a New Beginning* to help me with my new life in Christ.

NAME ______________________________

ADDRESS ______________________________

CITY ______________ STATE __________ ZIP __________

PHONE ( ) ______________ E-MAIL ______________

Mail To: **The Wisdom Center**
4051 Denton Hwy. · Ft. Worth, TX 76117
1-817-759-BOOK · 1-817-759-0300
You Will Love Our Website: WisdomOnline.com

Unless otherwise indicated, all Scripture quotations are taken from the King James Version of the Bible.
Seeds of Wisdom on Prosperity · ISBN 1-56394-089-2/B-22

Editor/Publisher: Deborah Murdock Johnson
Published by The Wisdom Center · 4051 Denton Hwy.· Ft. Worth, Texas 76117
1-817-759-0300 · 1-817-759-BOOK · **You Will Love Our Website: WisdomOnline.com**

Accuracy Department: To our Friends and Partners...We welcome any comments on errors or misprints you find in our book...Email our department: AccuracyDept@thewisdomcenter.tv. Your aid in helping us excel is highly valued.

DR. MIKE MURDOCK

- Has embraced his Assignment to Pursue...Proclaim... and Publish the Wisdom of God to help people achieve their dreams and goals.
- Preached his first public sermon at the age of 8.
- Preached his first evangelistic crusade at the age of 15.
- Began full-time evangelism at the age of 19, which has continued since 1966.
- Has traveled and spoken to more than 16,000 audiences in 40 countries, including East and West Africa, the Orient, Europe and South America.
- Noted author of over 200 books, including best sellers, *Wisdom for Winning*, *Dream Seeds*, *The Double Diamond Principle, The Law of Recognition* and *The Holy Spirit Handbook.*
- Created the popular *Topical Bible* series for Businessmen, Mothers, Fathers, Teenagers; *The One-Minute Pocket Bible* series, and *The Uncommon Life* series.
- The Creator of the Master 7 Mentorship Program, an Achievement Program for Believers.
- Has composed thousands of songs such as "I Am Blessed," "You Can Make It," "God Rides On Wings Of Love" and "Jesus, Just The Mention Of Your Name," recorded by many gospel artists.
- Is the Founder and Senior Pastor of The Wisdom Center, in Fort Worth, Texas...a Church with International Ministry around the world.
- Host of *Wisdom Keys with Mike Murdock,* a weekly TV Program seen internationally.
- Has appeared often on TBN, CBN, BET, Daystar, Inspirational Network, LeSea Broadcasting and other television network programs.
- Has led over 3,000 to accept the call into full-time ministry.

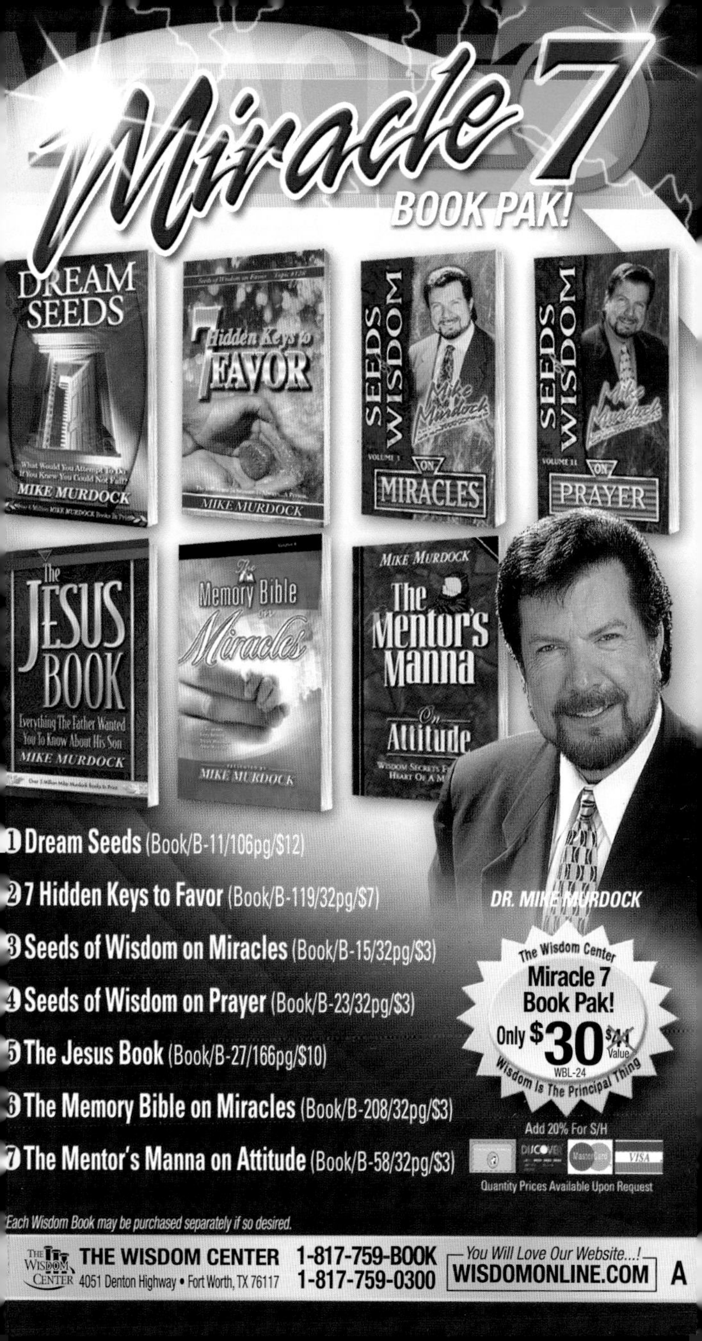

Miracle 7
BOOK PAK!
DREAM SEEDS
What Would You Attempt To Do If You Knew You Could Not Fail?
MIKE MURDOCK
7 Hidden Keys to Favor
MIKE MURDOCK
SEEDS of WISDOM
Mike Murdock
VOLUME I
ON
MIRACLES
SEEDS of WISDOM
Mike Murdock
VOLUME II
ON
PRAYER
The JESUS BOOK
Everything The Father Wanted You To Know About His Son
MIKE MURDOCK
The Memory Bible on Miracles
MIKE MURDOCK
MIKE MURDOCK
The Mentor's Manna
On
Attitude
DR. MIKE MURDOCK
1 Dream Seeds (Book/B-11/106pg/$12)
2 7 Hidden Keys to Favor (Book/B-119/32pg/$7)
3 Seeds of Wisdom on Miracles (Book/B-15/32pg/$3)
4 Seeds of Wisdom on Prayer (Book/B-23/32pg/$3)
5 The Jesus Book (Book/B-27/166pg/$10)
6 The Memory Bible on Miracles (Book/B-208/32pg/$3)
7 The Mentor's Manna on Attitude (Book/B-58/32pg/$3)
The Wisdom Center
Miracle 7
Book Pak!
Only $30 $41 Value
WBL-24
Wisdom Is The Principal Thing
Add 20% For S/H
Quantity Prices Available Upon Request
Each Wisdom Book may be purchased separately if so desired.
THE WISDOM CENTER
THE WISDOM CENTER 4051 Denton Highway • Fort Worth, TX 76117
1-817-759-BOOK
1-817-759-0300
You Will Love Our Website...!
WISDOMONLINE.COM
A

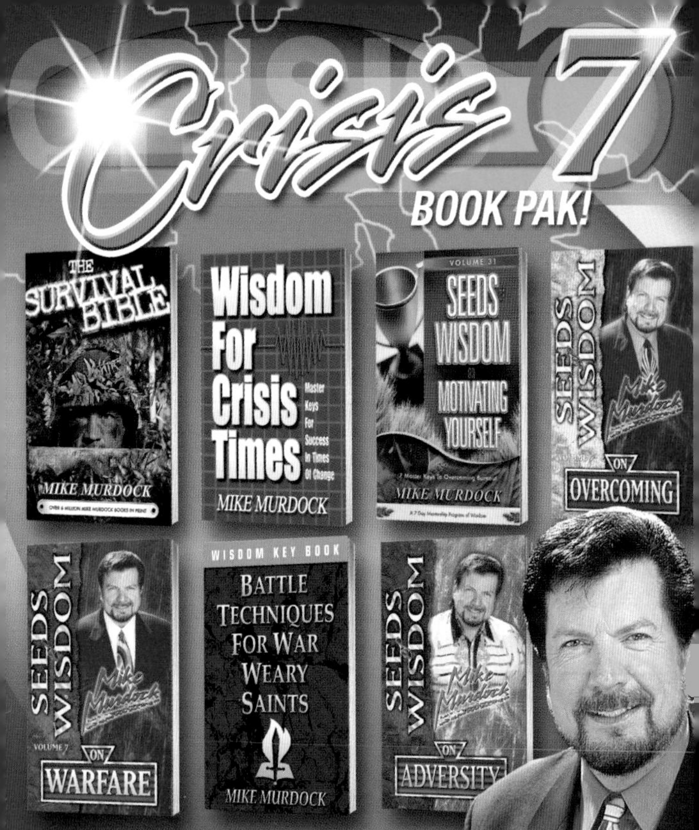
Crisis 7
BOOK PAK!
THE SURVIVAL BIBLE
MIKE MURDOCK
Wisdom For Crisis Times
Master Keys For Success In Times Of Change
MIKE MURDOCK
VOLUME 31
SEEDS OF WISDOM ON MOTIVATING YOURSELF
MIKE MURDOCK
SEEDS OF WISDOM ON OVERCOMING
Mike Murdock
SEEDS OF WISDOM ON WARFARE
VOLUME 7
Mike Murdock
WISDOM KEY BOOK
BATTLE TECHNIQUES FOR WAR WEARY SAINTS
MIKE MURDOCK
SEEDS OF WISDOM ON ADVERSITY
Mike Murdock

Career 7

Book Pak For Business People!

DR. MIKE MURDOCK

1. **The Businessman's Topical Bible** (Book/B-33/384pg/$10)
2. **31 Secrets for Career Success** (Book/B-44/114pg/$10)
3. **31 Scriptures Every Businessman Should Memorize** (Book/B-141/32pg/$3)
4. **7 Overlooked Keys To Effective Goal-Setting** (Book/B-127/32pg/$7)
5. **7 Rewards of Problem Solving** (Book/B-118/32pg/$7)
6. **Seeds of Wisdom on Productivity** (Book/B-137/32pg/$5)
7. **The Mentor's Manna on Achievement** (Book/B-79/32pg/$3)

The Wisdom Center
Career 7 Book Pak!
Only $30 ~~$45~~ Value
WBL-27
Wisdom Is The Principal Thing

Add 20% For S/H

*Each Wisdom Book may be purchased separately if so desired.

D

THE WISDOM CENTER
4051 Denton Highway • Fort Worth, TX 76117
1-817-759-BOOK
1-817-759-0300

You Will Love Our Website...!
WISDOMONLINE.COM

The Businessman's Devotional 4 *Book Pak!*

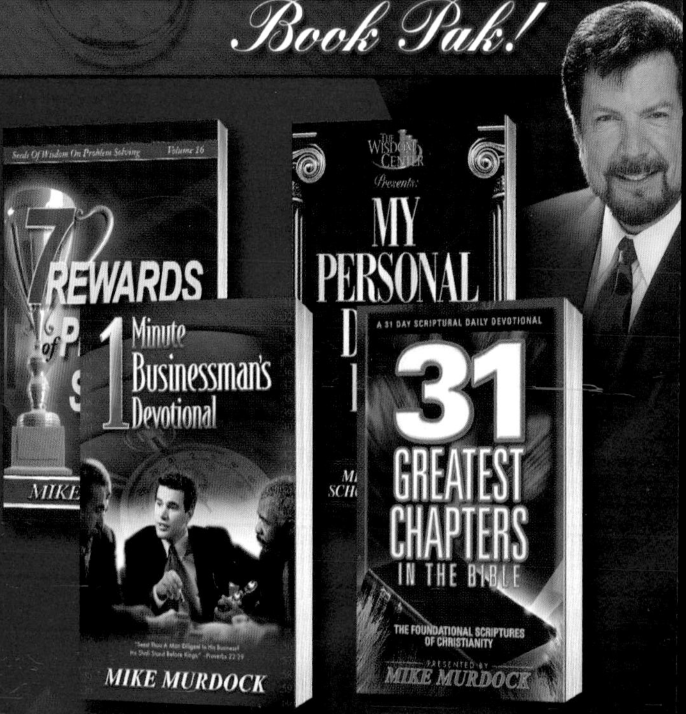

1. **7 Rewards of Problem Solving** (Book/B-118/32pg/$7)
2. **My Personal Dream Book** (Book/B-143/32pg/$7)
3. **1 Minute Businessman's Devotional** (Book/B-42/224pg/$12)
4. **31 Greatest Chapters In The Bible** (Book/B-54/138pg/$10)

The Wisdom Center
The Businessman's Devotional 4 Book Pak!
Only **$20** ~~$36~~ Value
PAK-22
Wisdom Is The Principal Thing

**Each Wisdom Book may be purchased separately if so desired.*

Add 20% For S/H

F **THE WISDOM CENTER** 4051 Denton Highway • Fort Worth, TX 76117 **1-817-759-BOOK** **1-817-759-0300** *You Will Love Our Website...!* **WISDOMONLINE.COM**